Blood Lines

Blood Lines

Poems by

Ann Bookman

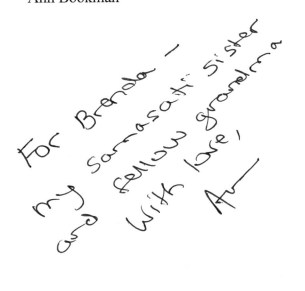

For Brenda —
my samasati sister
and fellow grandma
with love,
Ann

Cover Design by Shay Culligan
Cover Image by Kay WalkingStick, *April Contemplating May,*
Collection of the Whitney Museum of American Art, 1972,
50" x 50", acrylic on canvas.
Photo credit: Lee Stalsworth, www.artshooter.com

Library of Congress Control Number: 2022932934
ISBN: 978-1-63980-069-8

Kelsay Books
502 South 1040 East, A-119
American Fork, Utah 84003
Kelsaybooks.com

For my mother
Ruth Lowe Bookman
And my foremothers, known and unknown,
May their memory be a blessing

Acknowledgments

My thanks to the editors of Finishing Line Press who supported my work with the 2012 publication *Point of Attachment*. The following poems, with some variations, first appeared in that chapbook:
    "Clay"
    "Going Out"
    "Learning to Float"
    "Peonies"
    "Sight Seeing Trip"
    "Shimmering"
    "Teshuva: Turning and Return"

My thanks for permission to reprint previously published poems:

Valparaiso Poetry Review: "When Light Leaves"
Chronogram: A Journal of Arts, Culture and Spirit:
    "Constellations"
Soul-Lit: A Journal of Spiritual Poetry: "Impenetrable Blue" and
    "Hymn to Be Sung at Astronomical Twilight"
Dogwood: A Journal of Poetry and Prose: "The Accident"

A special word of gratitude to my inspiring teachers at the Fine Arts Work Center in Provincetown, MA. A number of poems in *Blood Lines* were either begun or revised in one of their classes. The magic of those intense discussions and revelatory moments animates this collection. My deep appreciation to Martha Rhodes, Gabrielle Calvocoressi, Gail Mazur, David Rivard and Major Jackson.

This book was birthed and nurtured by the La Dee Dah's writing group that met from 2010-2016. I want to thank Nancy Sommers and Carol Stack for their insightful comments on early drafts. I want to acknowledge the wisdom, encouragement and love I received from the group's founder, Sandra Morgen (1950-2017). She was my first professional collaborator, my model of intersectional feminist scholarship and activism, my soul sister: may she rest in power and in peace.

To my friends who have supported my journey into writing poetry by reading this manuscript and/or discussing the issues that birthed this collection, my sincere thanks: Andrea Cousins, Polly Allen, Carol Conaway, Susan Levin, Carol Michael, Mary Murphree, Arlene Pressman, Paula Rayman, Gail Reimer and Mary Wright. I also want to thank the members of my Women's Study Group for their sisterhood and support which began at Temple Israel in Boston over 30 years ago: Joyce Antler, Ellen Fishman, Fran Godine, Louise Lowenstein, Pamela Paternoster, Susan Porter, Frances Putnoi, Joan Rachlin and Rabbi Elaine Zecher.

To my family whose love and support make my life and poetry possible, my unending gratitude: to my husband and life partner, Eric Buehrens, for his love, wisdom and humor; to my children Nick Buehrens and Emily Buehrens McCarthy who have both faced unexpected health challenges with a bravery and resilience that is inspiring; and to my grandchildren, Jacob Douglas Buehrens and Dylan Joseph McCarthy, for the boundless joy they bring into my life every day.

To my brother, Richard Bookman, I give my heartfelt appreciation. His name does not appear in these poems, but he has been my mainstay in navigating our family journey–always there to celebrate the joyful milestones, to honor the ancestors, to lend a helping hand.

Finally, this collection would not exist in its present form were it not for the generous guidance and exquisite poetic sensibility of Fred Marchant. His questions and commentary unearthed levels of meaning that would otherwise have remained hidden. He showed me a bridge that was wider than I knew, accompanied me on the crossing. To Fred, I give my deep and enduring appreciation.

Contents

I.

Oh, I have made myself a tribe
Out of my true affections,
and some of my tribe is scattered!
—Stanley Kunitz

Migration Routes

Bloodstreams channel a mystery, personal yet shared, transport

a heavy leather trunk—prophetic genes, spliced memories,

uninhabited dreams—across the salt slick ocean,

unrelenting wave slaps.

Invisible navigators confront turbulence,

make landfall, set up camp: tents sway, ropes fray.

Millions upon millions in flow, swim past Liberty incognito:

No one applied for entrance to my body.

Black Satchel

I have only one photograph of Rivka, my great grandmother on my mother's side. She wears a long dark dress, buttons from neck to waist, ruffle of lace covers her throat, wrists. She poses for the camera; the occasion is obscure. *Camera obscura,* the darkened box, pinhole of light, objects partially revealed, upside down.

Rivka stands alone behind a round table, white cloth with long fringe covering the top. On the edge of the table, a black satchel: she holds the handle with her left hand. She works as a midwife in her neighborhood, makes home visits to pregnant women and mothers with infants. This is her medicine bag; she carries alcohol swabs, suturing thread, needles, scissors, and a small silver flask of brandy.

Rivka, her husband Solomon, and their two small children, landed at Ellis Island in March 1893. Was this photograph taken before she boarded the Drezden, the steamer ship on which she travelled to America? Or was it taken later when she lived in a tenement on Broome Street in the Lower East Side?

Rivka died in childbirth at thirty—escaping the illnesses linked to the *Ashkenazi gene* [i]—never held her baby girl. I wonder who picked her daughter's Hebrew name, *Chaya*. I think of this motherless little girl, the grandma I never met, when we toast *L'Chaim* at family occasions.

According to the Torah, Rivka—Hebrew for Rebecca—was the second matriarch of the Jewish people. In the Song of Songs, Rivka is described, "As a rose among the thorns, so is my beloved among the daughters." The name Rivka comes from the Hebrew *ribhqeh*—"tie firmly, connection, a link"—although some scholars have translated it as "bind, trap, snare." In a book of biblical names, Rivka means "knotted cord." So many threaded lives to unravel.

Creation Myths

Idiotic things, the smell of bread,
secret spice, bland as Sunday,
dough rising, kitchen metaphysics,
mystic of the frying pan: only the freshest ingredients will do.

Men in long robes, paupers and prophets,
dusty angels, dark unveiling, expose the sacrament,
carve seven days into earth's bark:
planet birthed over millennia.

Sweat vigorously, stretch more,
strike a cymbal—reverberations
can free you—curse fear, reject
every mirage: insist on candlelight.

Only tell the truth, whisper in open ears,
bless the breath takers:
they were more,
more than their book of belief.

The Knotted Cord

Do genes swim in our blood, stroke after stroke, a circular loop?
            Haul themselves onto sail-less boats
            with no rudder, hunker down, wait
            for new passengers to climb aboard.

Do some doze in muscle cells, awakened by unwelcome dreams?
            Jostle, urge neighbors to maliciously gossip,
            uncontrollably divide or multiply,
            wreak havoc inside a cell cave.

Or do genes lead hooded monkish lives in our skin?
            Rising before dawn, a pious contemplative
            life cannot contain twisting helix wildness,
            something gone awry, impervious to prayer.

Whose fingers braided this cobra lanyard, this knotted cord?
            Fate crosses randomness, right under left,
            left makes a loop, right goes under
            and through: pull the strands tight.

Pattern revealed—high risk. Risk cannot be unwound;
            it binds, constrains.

A Reason Why

Wind rises before it falls
starlight travels from the past
dew bends the morning grass
rocks are creased, older than God.

Snow crystals shine then melt
tides pull and release
shells give birth to birds
stems come before the flower.

Leaves curl before they die
hollow trees are homes
rain can be gentle or hard
common dirt can bear our weight.

Is there a reason why
some children live, motherless?

White Satin Wedding Slippers

My grandmother Edith—the inspiration for my middle name—died of ovarian cancer at forty-one. The details of her illness, like so much family history, cocooned in half-truths. As a girl I was told she died of stomach cancer: reference to women's *private parts* was taboo.

Edith was the only member of her immediate family to be born in America, but not the only one to gravitate toward learning. She came from a long line of scholars and rabbis, graduated from Hunter College in 1915, the first woman in her family to earn a bachelor's degree. During World War I, she longed to be of use, trained to be an ambulance driver. She earned her uniform and Red Cross cap, but the war ended as she was to set sail for France. Her disappointment was brief: she met and married my grandfather, Joseph, in 1919.

In their wedding portrait, my grandfather wears a dark tail-coated tuxedo, black top hat, white carnation on his lapel, stands a step lower than the regal Edith. She poses elegantly in a long white dress, head to floor veil, a bouquet of lilies and ribbons cascading from her gloved hands, covered arms. The hemline of her dress falls in folds around her ankles, revealing her shoes.

I used to stare at that photograph, at those pointy shoes, trolling for a memory that was slow to surface. Edith saved the shoes, passed them down to my mother. My mother never mentioned where she got them, gave them to me for "dress up" days. She allowed me to put on evening gowns she no longer wore; pinned up the skirts so I would not trip as I waltzed from room to room. I was a lady-in-waiting, waiting for womanhood and my wedding, carefully balancing my six-year-old self in my grandmother's high-heeled white satin wedding slippers. I stood before the mirror in my parent's bedroom, admiring my grownup look, unaware whose shoes I walked in.

Talking To Bela Bartok

Your terrarium has restored order,
but you will never return.
The things we are known for
rarely tell the story of who we are.
And who we are is rarely a story
we know how to tell.

You knew rhythm before words,
wrote piano sonatas at nine,
collected old Magyar melodies
in the hill towns of Hungary, *shtetls* of Moldovia.
Your dissonant heart haunted,
pentatonic scales of Siberian plains.

Borders began shifting, glass breaking,
unholy days bled into unholy nights—
reluctant passage to New York
before escape routes closed. For years
your score sheets remained blank,
teatimes near Carnegie Hall, but no music.

In your small apartment you continued
collecting: folk tunes, plant specimens,
mica and minerals, insects eating dirt,
making tunnels, carrying eggs.

Handmade

Upward stroke of a sable brush,
my mother painted rouge just below her cheekbone,
feint of hand makes pale cheeks blush.

Dabbing perfume drops with pointer finger—
twice behind each ear—
the way her mother taught her.

My grandmother's sepia portrait always in place
on my mother's dressing table, altar of intimacy:
I never knew her. I know her face as I know my face.

Owner of the brass menorah, keeper of the family flame,
I imagine my grandmother's hands gathering sabbath light,
her first name, my middle name.

When I wear perfume for an evening out,
I dab with my pointer finger twice behind each ear.
What's in a name? I never knew her.

Stones Not Flowers

Extended family, knee-to-knee,
in a long black limousine to Queens.
Thousands of dead Jews lying side by side:
so little space between them, so much time to share.

We buried Joseph, my grandfather:
the rabbi chanted the Kaddish, family members mumbled along.
Frigid January air, each breath a small white cloud
to hide their ignorance of the ancient Aramaic blessing.

Before leaving my mother and I walked arm in arm,
as women did in the old country, read the inscription
on my grandmother's headstone—first my mother,
then me—dates never spoken aloud before.

We placed stones on the graves of our ancestors,
Jews do not leave flowers when visiting the dead:
as if we could grasp grief in the palm of our hands.

Jam With No Bread

Heavy maroon drapes unopened, oriental planter left dry,
white wicker porch chairs empty. My grandfather
averted his eyes from the pillows, fabric still dented
by the curve of their backs.

Her closet a vessel he could not board, he might drown
in her dresses, blouses, shoes and smell.
The silver-backed brush on her oak bureau—
so many strands of her still attached.

Without warning, he closed the house,
made hasty arrangements for the children.
A trip of unknown duration, his itinerary followed
their honeymoon to national parks.

The children moved next door, sleepless
nights under thin blankets. On a dare
they snuck out, found the familiar
back door of their home unlocked.

In the icebox, one jar of strawberry jam.
They ate jam with no bread, sweet spoonful
after spoonful, licking the curved silver clean:
still famished.

Impenetrable Blue

I was trying to write about the unreasonableness of God,
Abraham and Isaac—you know, father and young son—
how could He ask for that?
As a child I preferred National Geographic
to Bible stories: two priests, veiled by moonless night,
led three children up the rocky path of *Yu-yai-ya-ko,*
home of Incan mountain gods.

The eldest girl wore a white-feathered cap,
her brother carried a farm tool,
his twin sister grasped a tiny doll in each hand,
miniature shawls, finely woven threads,
berry red and the impenetrable blue of midnight.

Long hours the priests labored, digging graves,
lining them with provisions, with stones.
When the pit was deep, they placed dirt-stained hands
on small heads, shining black hair.
Pouring from a jug of *chica* beer, they pressed
the spout firmly to each set of lips.

Dreaming between worlds, they lowered the children
below ground, closed their eyelids for eternity.
Before departing, the priests tied strings
of pearly shells around each child's neck:
gifts from the sea for thirsty deities
dwelling in dry Andean peaks.

Birthright

When my body becomes a warzone
of fear, fatalism and bleak prediction,
I recall where I lived before I was born.

Rivka Leya Rabinovich Rozenfeld
my maternal great grandmother, 1866–1896

Edith Rosenfield Lowe
my maternal grandmother
November 4, 1896–October 15, 1937

Edith Rosenfield Lowe and Joseph Lowe
New York, NY, 1919

The Lowe children—Ruth Louise, Charles Upton
and Jeanne Rosalie—Mt. Vernon, NY, c. 1928

The family house at Arcady, a summer resort
Lake George, Hague, NY, c. 1930

II.

Life is the only way
to get covered in leaves
and to keep on not knowing
something important.
—Wislawa Szymborska

Gee-Gee

I spoke at her funeral, have no memory of being there.

My aunt Jeannie—her dark-eyed Mediterranean beauty and fierce intelligence attracted many suitors—died of metastatic breast cancer at forty-seven. It was on my birthday, in two more days she would have been forty-eight: we often shared a celebratory lunch. My mother's little sister, my big sister, almost. As a toddler, I named her *Gee-Gee*. As a teenager, I confided in her, things I would not dare tell my mother: she was never shocked.

She was a journalist, urban affairs expert, published a book: *Cities in A Race with Time*. It took seven years to research and write; no one in the family could fathom why producing one book would take so long. I understood. How difficult it was to tell the story of struggling American cities in the civil rights era—the fight against poverty and for decent housing—how a passion for writing could consume one for years.

I relished visits to her New York studio apartment off Third Avenue. The walls were covered in evocative travel posters from her trips to Europe and floor-to-ceiling shelves overflowing with her books. I kept many of them, a brown and white *Ex Libris* sticker bearing her name inside each front cover. Her middle initial was R. for Rosalie

—a name I always thought missing on our family tree. Only recently I came to understand her mother's intentions: she chose a middle name for her daughter close to her own mother's name—*Rivka*—"a rose among the thorns."

When my aunt discovered a lump in her breast—perhaps in 1970, I do not know—she told no one, procrastinated about seeking a doctor. The tumor was finally removed, but it was too late: cancerous cells had already left their natal home, made their migratory dance of death into her stomach. She died looking six months pregnant, but childless.

Or did she choose not to have children? Single by choice? My aunt's life—notably different than other women in my family or in her generation—opened a path of possibility shaped by writing, travel, sex, and romance. I never got to ask her about the thorns.

Lunar Seas

The moon hangs like a ripe
orange in a black orchard
with no trees.

Lunar seas without water,
only the hardened deposits
of lava flows:

Sea of Tranquility
Sea of Fecundity
Sea of the Edge.

What a conveniently distant planet
to house barren anxiety
fear of the unknown.

On the hidden surface,
unnamed massive seas
flooded by magma.

Once steaming, now frozen,
colder than ice. Volcanic fire fountains
spray hot sparks, searing holes where they land.

Rivka, Edith, Gee-Gee:
I name a lunar sea for each of them.

Endurance

Linguine con vongole
steamy soup of life
in a shallow
sea green bowl:
the once brittle
now flexible,
the once hidden
now exposed.

Shells discarded
but not empty:
a small white muscle
remaining—
once strong enough
to open and close
a house –
now the lone survivor,
refuses
to abandon home.

Don't Throw Bouquets

When romance was a song
from a Broadway musical, dancing
cheek to cheek the path to heaven,
a girl stood on the sidelines. She wore
her best skirt, clingy low-cut sweater,
saw her man *across a crowded room,*
could not make the first move.

But not me, I was a child of the 60's:
no bra, unshaven legs, hiking boots,
dangly earrings Made in India.
Smash monogamy, who wants to be trapped?
The summer of 1969, TJ and I drove to P'town,
rusting VW van, peace painted on both sides,
blue jeans hung low on skinny hips,
his T-shirt proclaimed "Make Love
Not War," I wasn't sure.

Fucking in his backseat bedroom,
tie dyed sheets, thin mattress,
he said he really wanted
to get to know me.
When I got home, took a long hot shower:
washed that man right out of my hair,
out of my dreams.

41

Visitation

Amagansett, Long Island

The summer of Hurricane Carol: waves
swallowed wind-shaped dunes, sea grass and all,
in hungry gulps. Salt water seeped under the front door
of our beach cottage: gingham dish towels, thick bath towels,
none enough to soak up the widening spool of water.

Hunker down, said my mother, *wait for the storm to pass.*
But I knew we were trapped: phone lines down,
electric lights out, comforting static of the ham radio
silenced. Our yellow and white Chevy Impala
floated down the driveway like a bath toy.

We lit candles, played card games all night, afraid
to let sleep steal our watch. I must have dozed off:
by morning the bay no longer an ocean—
flat pewter platter extending to the horizon—
as if someone had let the air out of a balloon.

Suddenly a murmuration of starlings
above the beach, sparkling,
then darkening the sky,
black undulating curtain of shining wings,
swooning, swooping in unison,
putting the hurricane to shame,
a feathering of grace:
inviting us to join the dance.

Gleaming

My mother Ruth was a sculptor—*not a sculptress,* she used to say—insisting on women's equality before second wave feminism. A Fine Arts major, she studied with Oronzio Maldarelli at Columbia—even the sound of her mentor's name evoked terra cotta patinas, Latin passion.

But she had eyes only for my father, their courtship a fast-paced, pulsating, post-World War II romance. The band played *"Kiss me once, kiss me twice, kiss me once again"* at the wedding where they met. It was October 1945, my father home less than two months from his ordeal as a prisoner of war in the Pacific: by April the following spring they were married, honeymooned in Cuba.

Refusing to abandon her desire for the artist's life, she used a small room off the kitchen of our Manhattan apartment for her studio. Clay portrait heads of children—the first sculpted while I sat on the kitchen table playing with my own lump of clay at age three—allowed her to sculpt and care for my brother and me: designing her version of 1950s stay-at-home motherhood.

After we grew up, she returned to the medium she first loved—stone —chiseling abstract forms from blocks of serpentine marble. Making rough surfaces smooth, smooth surfaces shine, dozens of graded sandpapers until the inner color emerged: mottled green gleaming.

By the fall of 1972, she no longer spent time in her studio. Diagnosed at forty-one, her battle with breast cancer a 12-year struggle she was determined to win. But the available artillery lacked precision: two surgeries, radiation, chemical agents. Never told that her breast cancer had metastasized, never told she was dying: my father thought he was protecting her. The day she died was the kind of *"merry-month of June"* day we used to sing about in our *acapella* duets: she would have insisted on sitting outside in the sunshine.

Shaking Steps

La Guardia Airport, June 17, 1973

Grabbing the metal

handrail

walking down

shaking stairs

my father's distant

silhouette moves

in slow motion

across the steaming

black tarmac.

His tall, lean

familiar shape

blurry, clear,

blurry again,

as the distance

between us

narrows.

Perhaps it is

not him:

he is supposed

to be at her bedside

in the hospital
where he has cared
for his patients
for decades,
where he cannot
save her.

He keeps walking
towards me
arms reaching out
his eyes lock
with mine:
I have missed
the moment
maybe the mark.
I was flying in
paths crossed
in midair:
my plane landed
she ascended
clouds parting.

Rock, Paper, Scissors

Malignant, not benign,
lymph nodes already invaded,
the start of a war:
she never enlisted.

> The surgeon failed to find clean margins
> as though she had transgressed,
> written outside the lines
> of her life.

At thirteen, no one I knew
had breast cancer. Her first Sunday morning
home from the hospital, she told me
what they had done to her.

> Doctors do things like that?
> Short sentences, jagged pauses,
> deep breaths: I was numb,
> she was forty-one.

Alone, scanning a catalogue from Saks,
staring at shapely young women modeling
black and white brassieres: wondering
if mine were big enough.

> I grabbed a scissors from my desk drawer
> cut out their breasts, one by one,
> page after page.

Bloodletting

From the Greek *hystera, womb,*
her womb,
from the Greek ektomia, cut out,
of her.

>Etymological roots grow,
>twist, burrow, tighten their hold,
>cannot explain or erase
>a scalpel cutting.

When she dressed, I pretended
not to see the long new-moon
scar low on her belly. No memory
of hospital visits.

>Decades later a homemade
>"Welcome Home" card
>recovered: one heart encircled,
>pink crepe paper flowers.

She walked slowly out
of her bathrobe into tweed wool skirts,
color-coordinated cashmere sweater sets,
the fabric of normalcy, threads of denial.

>A sacred space of origin,
>cut out, medical waste.
>A response in blood: my menses stopped.

Separate Shores

A Sunday stroll with my father,
on Madison Avenue, not our usual route,
we never went to his office on weekends.
It smelled: medicinal alcohol used before shots.

> My brother and I sat in black
> Bauhuas waiting room chairs,
> patients who did not know we were sick
> with anxiety.

A small growth on her thyroid, two months
of radiation, out-patient procedure,
unrelated to her surgeries: no solid ground,
shorelines fickle, dunes eroding.

> For my father, recurrence a tornado
> of cyclonic dreams, shattering
> personal hope, professional oaths;
> do no harm, treat for cure.

I offered silence, asked no questions,
our pact. A new clause added—without negotiation—
this conversation never happened.
I had joined the conspiracy.

> Stranded on separate shores,
> my mother and I played our assigned roles,
> few scripted lines.

Bare Branches

There is a problem, with my mother's breathing:
a cavity—between lung and membrane—
filling up with fluid. My father is measured,
words rehearsed, trapped

> between medical knowledge
> and desperation: he cannot lie
> about anatomical location, cannot name
> its cause, its culmination.

Late September, green leaves turn
to gold, resign to brown, fall
to the ground: temperatures dropping,
daylight fading.

> In an autumn photo, she stands by the edge
> of the pond at our country house,
> tree branches bare. Her body at an angle:
> she chooses not to face the camera.

She has reached the final stage,
shadows flicker, her face, her neck.
It is the only black and white
photograph I have of her.

Lost in Central Park

After my mother died
I could not say the word
dead: I had not seen her die.
It was possible she was still alive—

                maybe hiding (unlike her),
                traveling abroad (she would have told me).
                Had she wandered out of the hospital,
                gotten lost in Central Park? She could not

have walked out. The last time I saw her legs
they were not my mother's legs.
Muscles atrophied; small bundle of bones
loosely wrapped in a sagging skin sack.

                I saw them by accident—her blanket slipped
                before the nurse could catch it—
                so thin, like twigs you could break
                with your bare hands.

After she died, I tried to see her face,
but all I could see were her chicken bone legs:
they followed me
everywhere I went.

Museum of Natural History

All eight lumbered slowly toward us
dark grey hulking forms, deeply folded skin,
like heavy velvet curtains
framing a Broadway stage.

I wanted to show my father I was tall enough
to reach the toes of the baby elephant,
small trunk wrapping around
her mother's ankle.

We gazed at tall grasses that no longer grew,
gazelles frozen mid-step in the Serengeti plain.
At each diorama I stared, asked—*"Are they alive?"*
He answered, *"Once. Now they are dead."*

I did not believe they were dead. Eyes wide,
forcing myself not to blink, counting for sixty seconds,
waiting for movement, a sound, a swallow: they must be hungry.
I wanted to show my father I had not been tricked.

My father was always right
until he wasn't. And that was not
about stuffed animals in glass cases,
and I was not nine.

On those Saturday afternoons I never wanted to leave
the Serengeti Plain. The largest gazelle looked
straight into my eyes, *Don't leave me,*
stay after they turn off the lights.

Peekaboo Hair

When I was thirteen, hair parted, covering
one eye, my father called me Veronica Lake.
I did not like him to tease me, but loved
her name, syllables spilling out,
vowel sounds, open water.

Icon of the 1940s silver screen,
her blonde hair wavy-sexy-smooth.
I Wanted Wings, her breakthrough film,
a box office smash: audiences—drawn to her
polished ivory beauty—saw her soar, then dive.

Three children, four marriages,
a child born prematurely on the set—
only lived one week—or so the story goes.
No stranger to humiliation, losing contracts,
husbands, health, and love.

Covering one eye: my girlhood self could guess
at what she might be hiding—something fagile,
flapping, hovering, ephemeral.
Veronica's life ended at fifty: last seen perched
on her lonely bone legs, certain she could fly.

Elegy for the French Wallet

You cannot consider yourself a New Yorker
unless you have traveled the Seventh Avenue subway,
unless you know what it's like to stand so close to others
you can hear people popping gum inside their mouths,
unless you know how to grab the straps
without losing your balance, without breathing,
until the next stop.

You cannot consider yourself a New Yorker
unless you have visited the Met on a Sunday afternoon
to admire the collection of Egyptian art,
the reconstructed Temple of Dendur
the tomb of the female pharaoh Hapshetshup:
she wore a false beard to assert her authority.
You were scared to look directly
into that slim opening in the stone façade
to view the sarcophagus holding the queen's body,
because she might not be dead: she might be alive
eating the food they packed for her,
in case she got hungry, ever.

You know you are a New Yorker when you lose
something personal, something valuable,
on the subway by mistake, or maybe it was stolen,
you were never quite sure whether
it was your fault, the time you lost your wallet,
the one your mother bought you
on her spring trip to Paris, after her second surgery.
The one she picked out for you because
of the vermillion leather exterior, because
you exclaimed *RED* as your favorite color at age three.

You didn't discover the wallet was gone until
you reached for your keys, until
you were greeted by Frank the balding doorman,
who repeated at every opportunity, *I knew you*
when you were just a bit of a thing, and now
here you are, wearing stockings and heels.
You told him what happened,
what you thought happened,
he tried to console, but you already knew:
you would never find another French leather wallet,
so beautiful, so vermillion.

Listening to *Madame Butterfly* with My Father

I imagined her hair was jet black,
held by red lacquered sticks, cherry blossoms tinged
with pale pink hung down one side of her neck, a few petals
touching the valley created by her collar bone,
her face powered white with rice flour,
her lips a crimson bud,
the folds of her ivory wedding kimono held in place
by an embroidered purple and gold *obi,* her sash
exquisitely knotted and bowed at her back, her fan
sprinkled with orange poppies that cannot hide her blush
when she sees the man she will marry,
her adolescent heart has already been won
by the handsome American, Colonel Pinkerton,
who knows her name is *Cio-Cio-san,*
who has already fallen for her painted beauty, pinned her wings
to ensure her loyalty, does not know that she will bear his child
after he departs, that he will break her heart by marrying another,
that Butterfly will abandon their young son,
using the ancient dagger with engravings
on the pearl handle her father used before her,
refusing to be dishonored, the dagger ripping
through her gown, her blood staining the satin,
her small body falling noiselessly like a leaf in autumn.

The opera ended, my father—a doctor—paused
before lifting the needle gently off the record,
as if tending to an open wound,
as we listened to Puccini in the comfort
of a Sunday afternoon living room,
as Butterfly's arias haunted my girlish heart
as I wondered how my father listened, an opera
that took place in 1904 in a house by Nagasaki Bay,

many years before he was captured
on Corregidor in '42, before he was a POW
in Manila until August 1945.
Am I dishonoring him to feel
Butterfly's heartache of love and betrayal,
when he cannot speak of his own heartache,
when he pretends only to count to three in Japanese,
the number of rice bowls he was allowed a day,
when he whispers two Japanese words he was forced to say,
thank you, *arigato gozaimas,*
when he can only tell one story,
the day a stray cat wandered into the prison camp,
and he killed it, and he cooked it,
and he ate it?

Black Wing Tips

I am not allowed in her hospital room
that morning, the June sky
a searing blue blossom.

Nurses scurry in and out,
trays of medication, hoses, syringes, sponges:
has there been a leak?

Pink pleura, her lungs filling
with fluid for months,
they cannot stem the flood.

My father, a doctor, must be standing
close at her bedside—
I imagine he holds her paleness tenderly.

From my watch in the limey corridor, the plastic wall clock
ticks slowly relentlessly dragging each second
out to its maximum capacity, tenacity.

My father emerges, ignores my pleading
eyes, kicks the brutish wall—twice—
his black wing tips shrouded in white.

Out of the heart hole plaster dust flies everywhere:
wail notes stick in my throat, specks of soul.

Going Out

When she is dressing to go out,
I quietly enter my mother's room.
The slow smoothing of her stockings
observed for secret imitation,
the zipping of her formal gown
a ritual fascination. She beckons me
to fix her evening bag.

I know what must be done:
first the handkerchief, her collection
neatly pressed and folded in a blue satin bag
in the top dresser drawer. Some are monogrammed
and smell of a perfume sweet and familiar,
others a keepsake from her mother,
the grandma I never knew.
Which hankie should I pick tonight?
I linger over the decision
relishing the power I possess.

Then the lipstick and compact set,
pressed powder escaping
like fairy dust
from its sterling silver box.
Finally, the comb, sheathed
in a tortoiseshell case,
bejeweled by a rhinestone rabbit
with one winking ruby eye.

She was the most beautiful woman in the world,
and then she had to leave.
Sweet wishes for my dreaming,
stroking the seal trim on her evening wrap,
one hug at the open door.

Jeanne R. Lowe, my maternal aunt
April 30, 1924–April 28, 1972

Ruth Lowe Bookman, my mother
July 19, 1920–June 17, 1973

Ruth Lowe Bookman and John Jacob Bookman, MD
New York, NY, April 14, 1946

Joseph and Edith Lowe with Ruth, 1921, (top) John and Ruth
Bookman with Ann Edith, 1948, at Arcady

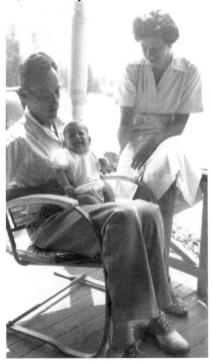

The Bookman family—Ruth, John, Ann and her brother Richard—
Central Park, NYC, 1954

III.

כל העולם כולו גשר צר מאוד עופרה חזה מילים: רבי נחמן מברסלב לחן: ברוך
חייט כל העולם כולו

The whole world is a narrow bridge:
the most important thing is not to be afraid.
—Rabbi Nachman of Breslov.

Scattered Tribe

I dreamt there was a band inside me,
one player bowed a bass larger
than herself, another blew
a brass horn on loan from an angel,
a third played flute—pursing
her lips, kissing each note
goodbye, lingering over some
like a lover—while children
followed her tunes, her blooms, lifted
off the ground by the music inside her magic.

I dreamt there was a parade inside me
pubescent girls carried helium balloons,
released sun-shafted rainbow streamers,
mothers stood on floats, waved
out windows of miniature houses,
held homemade signs of hope.
Ten grandmothers—all mine—
marched to the beat of a long-legged drummer,
held fast to their banner, both hands,
stitched letters of belonging, belief.

I prayed there was a fertile acre inside me
women tilled soil, planted seeds,
harvested maize, baked bread
with no yeast,
gathered kindling and firewood,
ensured the flame never died,
held a place open at every table
so all who are hungry could come and eat.
If summoned, I walk in a procession
of mourners, wail behind a wagon.

When Light Leaves

Drenched in sea glass
blue, cloud contours faintly drawn,
the artist's hand shakes;

hard to sketch
wisps of heaven.
Apricot skin sky seconds before

sunset, the orb slides silently
under the wave crests.
Colors deepen, myriad hues

and blues, there can never be
too many blues:
sea, sky, sea,

your eyes. Three grey clouds emerge,
stretch out lithely on an unseen shelf,
parallel to the measureless horizon.

One tiny white cloud,
top left corner from my perch
on the beach. A perfect triangle;

my line of sight the hypotenuse,
holding disparate pieces,
heart shards, splintering.

Protective Factors

I traverse a desert of hidden land mines, hear explosions that never occur. Tiptoe on eggshells, imagine cracks that never appear. Not maimed, not scarred: my 40s the worst. I name the entry into midlife the Double D—decade of diagnosis—recalling the ages of my foremothers.

I escaped all those years, imagining the worst when my children were young. Sick at heart, but not with the disease.

The chances are 50/50. I decide to be tested in 2006: The results confirm my fear. But I am the first woman on my maternal grandmother's side to live into my 60s in four generations, perhaps more. I feel no joy, cannot celebrate. Is resistance to good news genetically determined?

I ask my doctor, *"How can a woman with 'the gene' escape?"* Her research to find cases, control groups, causal relationships, is still in the early stages. She speaks slowly, *"You may have protective factors...We just don't know what they are."* Not her exact words, *"You may have a gene that turns off the BRCA gene. You may have a gene that promotes longevity."*

Protective factors—two words—a radical reframing of a picture neatly painted in black and white. Unsure where evidence of protection resides: I waver between the prosaic and holy. My *"high risk"* family history is not my destiny. The narrow bridge—the *Gesher Tsar Me'od*—we sing about in *shul* now stretches out for miles. Each verse is sung twice, the tune haunts me, holds me.

I know this bridge: I have been crossing it since I was thirteen, the year of my mother's mastectomy. It is an old rope bridge, slim wooden planks, connecting cables of braided vine. It sways with every step. I do not look down: refuse to be sucked under by the unruly current…or swallowed by the infectious whirlwind.

Hidden Treasure

Reeds, glassworts, cordgrass,
their reflections shine in shallow water,
saltmarsh decomposing as it flourishes.

I wait for the ephemeral
comforting softness of mud flats
reemerging as the tide retreats.

Fiddler crabs scurry in and out,
newly revealed holes. I want to peer
inside spaces where they molt,

travel in tunnels of transformation:
one body abandoned, another entered.

Thin Ice

The river appears motionless,
cold water bubbles and winds
beneath, numbs memory,
not fear. Distant black dots;
birds huddle, looking for home.

Temperatures rise, dive, rise:
repeat. At night a smooth glaze,
as if the river had been spun off a potter's wheel,
wet puddles in morning reflect the city skyline
mirror my longing for spring, for more time.

Fragile crystals, false moves, one foot
in front of another: do I dare
to release my weight?

Clay

Everyone said we looked alike,
I did not see the resemblance.

My mother kept clay moist under wet cloths,
wrapped short wooden sticks with copper wire—
butterflies she called them—
each pair attached to a sturdy metal frame.

In minutes the clay was up on the armature—
butterflies disappeared. My mother's eyes moved back
and forth, from clay-to-me-to-clay,
with wooden calipers she checked clay skull, clay face
against my skull, my face. Her face?

The smell of linseed oil on her tools lured me.
Friends of the family asked, *are you a sculptor too?*
No, I replied, wondering.
Old mirrors, new reflections,
I see my lips, nose, curls as she saw them:
see myself in her art,
the art in my life.

Georgica

East Hampton, Long Island, 1958

After dinner, I grab my shiny red Schwinn Starlet—
a present for my tenth birthday—
ignore my mother's sneaker rule,
power up Briar Patch Road
barefoot, feel the ridges of the pedals
on the soles of my feet.

I have my bike route: can shut my eyes,
know when to turn. Georgica Pond comes into view,
I call it the "lagoon of dreams,"
I read that in a book. I love to repeat the name
over and over: *Georgicaaah, Georgicaaaah,*
I wish my name was Georgica.

I take a right onto Blue Hydrangea Lane,
people say I have beautiful blue eyes,
but I don't even know if I am pretty.
Mansions bigger than our yard, honeysuckle bushes
so high you can barely see the houses,
I inhale, sweet scent like my Nana's perfume.

Left on Jericho Terrace, houses with hedges
carved into animal shapes—
there's is a word for this, I can't remember—
larger than life shadows of rabbits and deer.
They might come alive and chase me,
but I have my bike, make my escape.

The next road is a steep climb:
I stand on the pedals, rise up
and up, panting, sweating,
my palms slippery on the handles.

The top of the hill is the prize,
afterwards the long, long, lovelee ride down.

Here I go: no pedaling now
cool wind fills my shirt like a kite
wheels spin on their own
feet off the pedals
hands off the breaks
so fast, faster than fireflies:
I'm a firefly with my own light.

I sing loudly, make up a song
about the wind and my bike
and the hedge animals hiding
in the honey suckle night.

Teshuva: Turning and Return

In a synagogue of strangers
I said the Kaddish prayer:
I was a mourner without *minyan*
when my mother died.
The words meant nothing, sounds everything,
the chanting of ancient Aramaic
slid stealthily into prayerless nights.

In a thicket of ignorance I wandered
unable to read a prayer book in Hebrew.
As a girl, I hid the names of my ancestors,
dismissed their language,
straightened my hair.
Saturday mornings we visited my grandfather,
I thought the Sabbath was Sunday.

On the morning of Yom Kippur,
the call to prayer shaped
the landscape of my wilderness,
my narrow place. I sought water
found only a dry riverbed: swirling patterns
of sand held the memory of water,
no relief for my thirst.

When will I admit my own longing,
or speak aloud my first prayer?
I pray to cast away shame.

Peonies

I have no praise for pink-petalled masses,
prefer the tight-fisted buds.

Black ants circle the hard waxy surface:
there is no honey to suck.

It is not the ant that seeks sustenance from the flower,
but hidden carpels that listen for tapping of tiny insect feet.

The moment before the bloom
holds the real romance.

The imprint of tender repeated gestures begins
the unfurling of the first petal, the unfolding;

I let my eyes rest in your gaze
more than a fleeting moment.

Sight Seeing Trip

When my mother died I went west with the man
I loved but could not marry. We kept missing the scenic routes,
roadmaps outdated and torn. Drove too long each day—
only cheap hotels still had *OPEN* signs after midnight.

That night our motel room was shadowed
and shabby. I lay partly clothed under the bedspread,
not between the sheets, fearing
the fall into sleep.

And then my mother came to me,
her hair filled with leaves and pears,
her eyes clear through layers
of wallpaper, paste and plaster.

She spoke calmly from the other side
of the wall, of the world,
of loving and losing,
and I knew where she was,
among the leaves and the pears
of the wall-world.

From Manchester to Stoke on Trent

Spring exists; I had reason to doubt.
Sturdy stone cottages, lazy sheep grazing
no particular plan, green reappears

lacking an invitation. Branches thicken
expectantly, buds bulge from memory,
a fragrance fills my nostrils unannounced.

From the train window, a canal loops into sight,
the white bodies of two swans
reflected in black water, necks intertwined.

The Accident

Taconic Parkway, Beacon, NY, 1988

I never saw his car:
the mangled metal.

I saw the tree
cracking in two
upon impact,
opening itself, not falling,
creating a path
upward, its bark revealing
the circle lines of time.
He ascended the tree trunk
at a ninety-degree angle
defying gravity
his arms stretched out
the bare upper branches
were the last earthly thing
his fingers touched
before he flew,
wingless,
into the great cradle bowl of souls.
My father passed over
to the other side
of the Hudson River,
his last breath audible
only to nuthatches and cardinals
building new nests in the treetops,
sturdy cups of mud and feathers,
dried grass, crooked twigs:
it was the first day of spring.

Reach, Fall, Fathom

I.

Paddling a canoe,
pond of lily pads: flower,
flat, open, closed.

Ivory comb from Nana
falls from my knapsack, sinks,
the muddy bottom.

Arm in dark water—
a flash of white bone beneath—
stretch, stretch, beyond reach.

Water lilies bloom briefly,
my girlhood slipping away.

II.

Open air shower
warm water caressing,
outside when inside.

Silver bubbles catch
the light—snake silently down
my skin—shine, vanish.

Slippery stone tiles,
I fall: attempt surrender,
refuse to return home.

What is poisoning my well?
I fear seepage through the soil.

III.

A seaward journey,
I pack lightly, wait barefoot
on a slim shoreline.

An empty vessel,
no oars, no anchor, hull
slices water, waves open.

Motion of wave crests,
buoyed, pillows of sea foam,
I rest my head.

The ocean floor is a matter of faith…

Ruth Lowe on the balcony of the Museum of
Modern Art where she worked, 1942–48

Ruth Lowe Bookman sculpting a portrait head,
Bucks County, PA, 1968.

Jeanne Lowe at Piazza San Marco, Venice, c. 1950

Jeanne Lowe, author photo from her book
Cities in a Race with Time, 1967

IV.

...It seems I am on the edge of discovering the green notebook containing all the poems of my life. I mean the ones I never wrote. The meadow turns intensely green. The notebook is under my fingers.

—Jane Cooper

Learning to Float

It was magical, but physical:
the weight of a human body
suspended on the sea surface.
Water one can dive into,
hold your breath, pretend
to disappear. Water
one can skip stones over,
watch them flip, jump, sink.

My mother knew how to float.
We started our lessons in shallow water,
her strong hands supporting
my reluctant five-year old back.
Stretch out your arms,
pretend to be an angel in the snow.
Each day her hands eased out
to a different position.

That day I felt the tips of her fingers
touch the edges of my rib cage.
That day I lay effortlessly atop
the gentle waves of Amagansett Bay,
caught off guard
by my own power.

I missed the final moment of release.

But Not This

My peach sweet girl, curly chestnut hair, smile that lights up a room, rocking her in the dark, "you are my sunshine."

I remember waiting for test results when she lived in utero: was a healthy baby was growing inside me? Weeks and weeks of waiting. The doctor's handwritten note on an Rx pad, *"Congratulations— it's a girl!"* In the photo album of her first year, I pasted the grainy, grey sonogram taken when we first heard her heart, first saw her teeny right hand, arm stretching out.

Now my daughter sits by my side: different doctor's office, different exam room. She is twenty-five years old. She has decided to be tested, but I am not ready to know. She says, *"Mom, you always say knowledge is power."* Did I say that? I forgot to tell her I am not brave: she is.

They have taken eight vials of her blood: her results are inscribed on waxy white paper, tiny indelible black markings, upside down. The doctor's eyes hold regret before she speaks. I hear words, not sentences: *high risk, prophylactic surgery, Ashkenazi Jews, life-long implications.*

Four letters and one number spin with uncanny accuracy into the bull's eye, my daughter's body. Her face in profile, deep red spreads, her neck, her cheek; capillary branches appear, rising pulse waters cannot be dammed.

L'dor Va Dor, from generation to generation. I want my grandmother's brass menorah with the lions of Judah standing on their hind legs, her silver spice box, her engraved Shabbat candlesticks, but not this.

I want my daughter to inherit my green thumb, the serpentine marble sculpture my mother carved, my *Child's First Book of Verse*—with page corner turned down for "The Lamplighter"—but not this.

Morning Ritual

I like the water hot
streams rivering my back
arms stretch out across the shower stall
hands grasp a smooth marble shelf
heels press against the opposite wall;
I am a bridge unto myself
connecting the divided parts.

I rise up on my toes three times,
Kadosh, kadosh, kadosh.
Holy, holy holy:
allow myself one word
close to hope.

From My Study Window

Few cars venture down my dead-end road,
spring rain carves rivulets in the dirt, deep gullies
along the edge, like toothless lips of an old woman
who knows all, hums quietly, tells nothing.

The shadow of death shelters
in the bones of an elderly neighbor,
he awaits the arrival of his daughters,
their names no longer known to him.

Illness invades the young wife next door,
she holds fast to her shield of confidence,
her left breast lost, her hair grown
back now, curly as parsley.

A scarlet tanager flies daringly close to my window,
calling attention to the moment,
early morning light curves over sturdy pines
spills gently onto my blank page.

Constellations

Orion's belt shines in three-point precision
as we huddle, eyes raised,
in the frigid, crystalline air.
Even the Pleiades have shed
their hazy filaments, rejoined
the company of breathing lights.

Clearness is not about seeing:
I want to lie with you—folded,
silent, barely sleeping. I want
the glow of meteors to course
through our veins, the slow
reflected glory of light years
to extend our time.

Hold me again, as on a February night
by Provincetown harbor,
fill the sky with Latin names,
animal heads, gods and ghosts.
Undress me with assurance,
make the surface of my skin
a celestial map—
one unknown sun—discovered.

Restoration

Y*arzheit* visit to the field, afraid to look for ashes.

This was the place we chose: comforting arms
of old stone walls, knee-high grasses, open sky.
The field sloped down to a massive rock slab,
upended in the ice age.

I remember the first year, my father did the deed.
He stood in shaded cool of leafy branches,
dappled light, his arm a sweeping arc,
sowing the seeds of a lifetime.

A year has passed, in a trundle of rotting leaves
a single day lily grows—deep orange petals,
butter-yellow center, jet-black stamens—
sways on a slender stalk.

A restoration of color: she has joined the cycle of seasons.

Improvisation

If jazz brings tears, do not hide
don't sweep away minor keys
don't tear out pages of self-flagellating journals
don't censor the lines you wish you never wrote
the lie you confessed to yourself, but not to me.
Every cup of coffee contains a conversation,
a renovation, cracked saucers, coded messages.

Remember your Mad Max motorcycle days?
Wrapping my sunburned arms
around your chest, bumpy off-road rides
driving fast, driving crazy fast,
over ruts, rocky turf,
falling off—intentionally—splashing
in cool sundrenched creeks, till we were so wet
we had to take our clothes off:
we didn't know what we had.

Vocation

Physicians (not doctors),
paleographers, chemists,
English teachers, cloth merchants,

real estate investors, rabbis:
men are professionals, women volunteer.
Not one is a poet.

The globe of expectation
never stops turning, rotates
at an unexpected angle.

The pointer finger touches the thumb,
the needle is held firmly,
thread pulled tightly.

The men wear tailored suits,
the women sew, stitch and mend,
their work is done, undone.

If I lived in another century, another body,
would my fingers hold a pen?
Words forming, flying out.

Acqua Alta

Arms around backs
legs across hips
our signature tangle:
you tell me about your dream.
You are driving through water
something heavy falls out
you make a wrong turn
cannot find a map.

The *acqua alta* rises
at your Venetian doorstep
last year's high-water mark
has disappeared. You navigate
narrow channels, perhaps
the canals you crossed
each misty morning
to a small café on the *Vetere,*
sipping the balm of solitude
letting go of anger, being kinder
to yourself.

In your dream riverbanks slide away,
you ask me, *what is water than never ends?*
An infinity pool. Yes!
I give you two words,
want to give you more.
You shawl me in reverie:
we inhale, skin on skin, wordlessly.

Simplicity

Paring down, bearing down:
cut hours from my workweek
miles from my commute.
File cabinets overflow, field notes, book chapters,
typed drafts, white out: my children
never owned typewriters.

My closet bulges with work suits,
pocketbooks, heels to match. I promise
bags for Goodwill and Rosie's Place,
cannot part with a handmade Norwegian sweater
garment from another tribe: my hair is dark,
curly, kinky, not blond, never straight.

At sixty, I no longer yearn for an "e"
at the end of my name.
If I had one, I'd throw it away.

Hiking the Mountains of Moab

Grand Junction, Colorado

A woman alone in the desert,
a familiar fear, brush away cobwebs of *what if.*
The trail is steep, muscles in my legs
begin to ache: I am walking, working, climbing.

Without warning, a loud sound: large rocks falling,
a change in the weather, sleeping boulders grinding together?
I cannot name it: cannot quell the urge
to label it, to claim it.

The path curves and slivers, tiny wildflowers
nestle in rock crevices, fuchsia and white,
deep red, blood orange. I pretend the palette of petals
relieves the tightness in my chest.

I continue to climb: in my mind I am turning
back, in my heart I am moving forward to find
the fossilized plants, discover the dinosaur bones,
peer into pits where archaeologists labored.

A large lizard darts across my path, the tightness
in my chest moves down my legs. Ascending
onto a flat rock, the lizard ignores my presence,
pink tongue licks the air.

Colors pull me closer: skin bright turquoise,
neck encircled in black, head crowned in gold:
my heart pounds, the lizard's belly moves
rhythmically in-out, in-out.

The lizard's breathing, my own breathing,
a quickening of awe: *Baruch atah...*

What We Carry

For Nick, August 2018

Blanket, a soothing word,
blanket, like the warm handmade quilt
sewed for your crib when you were born,
a scatter of stars, one banana moon,
stitched into the indigo blue
of your dreams.

You carried it from room to room,
used it as a pillow on your first bed
until you left it somewhere,
never asked to find it:
you were ready to live
without your blanket.

But I was not ready for you to leave
when you moved to the other side
of the Continental Divide, slept
on a portaledge suspended
from a cliff side, sailed alone in Puget Sound
in a small wooden boat that leaked.

In three months you will become a father,
you will love your child more than life,
your heart will break, you will forgive:
it will be hard to understand,
in time you will.

Shimmering

It was a humid summer night
ground fog shimmering
with Adirondack nostalgia
and morsels of regret,
when she alighted
on the turreted roof top
of the Lake George house.
She moved quickly, gracefully,
pausing on the wide front porch,
pale yellow pillars wrapped
in heart-shaped leaves
and plump purple grapes.

Freeing herself from
fruited vines, lowering
herself down
through narrow spaces
that open and close
like the gills of a fish:
she swam out through
the markings of memory,
releasing fugitive sighs
that were no longer
breath, her arms extending
for miles, enfolding me,
holding me, giving me a face
I can recognize—hers—
and a place to inhabit
as myself.

Hymn To Be Sung at Astronomical Twilight

Lichen, all that remains green, clings
to the naked stump. One piece of bark
lingers in the dirt,
survived the shredding,
only to be trapped
between decay and salvation.

I heard it howl
when they split the trunk into billets,
heard the crass conquering laughter
of the hatchet men when they first saw
the wet sapwood in the middle:
you'd think they'd *discovered* America.

But you and I know
that tree had no more chance of living
among the rotting flesh
of humans and mammals—
or the underbellies of ancient sea creatures—
than any of us.

If you think it's hard
to make out shapes and sense
from decaying dirt, then wait
till your eyes are used to the dark:
you will see animal hearts and the skins of ghosts
you will see tender shoots and saplings,
a grove of saplings,
like far off stars
waiting to be born
waiting for the light.

Ann Bookman and her daughter, Emily Ruth, Wellfleet, MA, 1987
and Jackson Corners, NY, 2020

Flight Forms, cast aluminum, 1970,
by Ruth Lowe Bookman

Notes

The prose poem "Black Satchel" refers to the "Ashkenazi gene." This is one of two genetic mutations known as BRCA 1 and BRCA 2, both of which lead to an elevated risk of breast cancer and ovarian cancer. Discovered in 1994, this genetic mutation is more prevalent among Jewish women from Eastern and Central Europe than from other ethnic/religious subpopulations. (See "Genetics of Breast Cancer" by M.H. Greene, 1997)
https://www.mayoclinicproceedings.org › article › fulltext

The prose poem "Gee-Gee" refers to a book written by my aunt, Jeanne R. Lowe, *Cities in a Race with Time: Progress and poverty in America's renewing cities* (Random House, 1967).

Quotations from the following authors appear as epigraphs in this collection: Stanley Kunitz, "The Layers" in *The Wild Braid; A poet reflects on a century in the garden* (Norton, 2000); Wislawa Syzmborska, "The Note" in *The New Yorker* (November 28, 2005); Jane Cooper, "The Green Notebook" in *The Flashboat: Poems Collected and Reclaimed* (Norton, 2000).

The words to the song "Kol Ha'Olam Kulo" are attributed to Rabbi Nachman of Breslov. Translation courtesy of www.aish.com

This collection contains occasional words or phrases in Hebrew. These can be translated as follows:

Baruch Atah—the beginning of many prayers to Adonai [God], literally "Blessed Art Thou…."
L'Chaim—a toast offered at life cycle events meaning "to life."
Kaddish—a hymn of praise to God, a prayer spoken by mourners at a burial or yahrzeit.
Teshuva—repentance, one element of atoning for sin in Judaism.
Yahrzeit—the anniversary of someone's death, especially a parent.

About the Author

Ann Bookman is a poet, anthropologist and social justice advocate. She has been studying poetry for twenty years with Boston area poets and in residential workshops at the Fine Arts Work Center in Provincetown, MA. Her poems have been published in *Chronogram, Larcom Review, Soul-Lit: A Journal of Spiritual Poetry* and *Dogwood: A Journal of Poetry and Prose*, among others. In 2012 she published a chapbook, *Point of Attachment,* with Finishing Line Press. *Blood Lines* is her first full collection.

Bookman's career has been bookended by positions focused on women's creativity, potential and power. Early in her career she served as Associate Director of the Bunting Institute at Radcliffe College working with an interdisciplinary group of women scholars, writers and artists. From 2013 through 2018, she was Director of the Center for Women in Politics and Public Policy at UMass Boston weaving an intersectional feminist perspective into her teaching, research and activism.

Bookman received a BA from Barnard College and a PhD in social anthropology from Harvard University and held research and teaching positions at MIT, Brandeis University and the College of the Holy Cross. A nationally known scholar and policy expert in women's issues, work/family balance and community engagement, she is the co-author with Sandra Morgen of *Women and the Politics of Empowerment* (Temple University Press) and the author of *Starting in Our Own Backyards: How working families can build community and survive the new economy* (Routledge).

She also worked in government as a Presidential Appointee during the Clinton administration serving as Policy and Research Director of the Women's Bureau at the US Department of Labor.

Bookman is currently a Senior Fellow at the McCormack Graduate School of Policy and Global Studies at UMass Boston and serves on the Board of the Hudson Valley Writers Center. Born and raised in Manhattan, she lives in Boston and Columbia County, NY with her husband, Eric Buehrens.